LIVES
AND
TIMES

Walt Disney

Wendy Lynch

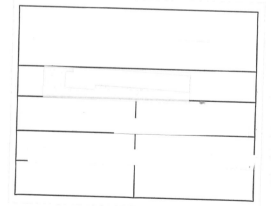

Heinemann
LIBRARY

First published in Great Britain by Heinemann Library
Halley Court, Jordan Hill, Oxford OX2 8EJ,
a division of Reed Educational and Professional Publishing Ltd.
Heinemann is a registered trademark of Reed Educational & Professional Publishing Limited.

OXFORD FLORENCE PRAGUE MADRID ATHENS
MELBOURNE AUCKLAND KUALA LUMPUR SINGAPORE TOKYO
IBADAN NAIROBI KAMPALA JOHANNESBURG GABORONE
PORTSMOUTH NH (USA) CHICAGO MEXICO CITY SAO PAULO

Designed by Ken Vail Graphic Design, Cambridge
Illustrations by Donald Harley
Printed in Hong Kong / China

02 01 00 99 98
10 9 8 7 6 5 4 3 2 1

ISBN 0 431 02486 3

Some words are shown in bold, **like this**. You can find out what they mean by looking in the glossary. The glossary also helps you say difficult words.

British Library Cataloguing in Publication Data

Lynch, Wendy
Walt Disney. - (Lives & times)
1. Disney, Walt, 1901–1966 - Juvenile literature 2. Animators - United States - Biography - Juvenile literature 3. Motion picture producers and directors - United States - Biography - Juvenile literature
I. Title
791.4'3'023'092

Acknowledgements

The Publishers would like to thank the following for permission to reproduce photographs:

Aquarius Library/Walt Disney Co: pp10,18, 19; James Davis Travel Photography: p17; John Frost Newspaper Library: p20; Chris Honeywell: p21; Wendy Lynch: p22; Robert Opie Collection: p11; Popperfoto: p23; Spectrum Colour Library: p16

Cover photograph reproduced with permission of Walt Disney Co/The Ronald Grant Archive.

Our thanks to Betty Root for her comments in the preparation of this book.

Every effort has been made to contact copyright holders of any material reproduced in this book. Any omissions will be rectified in subsequent printings if notice is given to the Publisher.

Contents

The first part of this book tells you the story of
Walt Disney.
The second part tells you how you can find out
about his life.

Early life

Walt Disney was born in America in 1901.
At school, he liked art best. He liked
drawing **cartoons**.

When he was 18, Walt started to work for a company that made films. In the evenings he made his own cartoons at home. He called these cartoons 'Laugh - O - Grams'.

Cartoons

Walt drew lots of pictures and took photos of them. When the photos were joined up into film and played, the pictures looked as if they were moving. This is called **animation**.

In 1923, Walt moved to Hollywood to make **cartoons**, with his brother Roy. They bought an old building and called it the Walt Disney **Studio**. This is how the Walt Disney Company began.

Mickey Mouse

In 1928, Walt and a friend, called Ub, made a cartoon character called **Mickey Mouse**. Mickey Mouse became very famous. So did his friends Minnie Mouse, Donald Duck, Pluto and Goofy.

The first two Mickey Mouse cartoons were
silent. Walt worked very hard to find out
how he could have sound in his films. Soon
he learned how to use his own voice for
Mickey Mouse.

Colour

Films were made in black and white because people did not know how to make films in colour. In 1932, film makers began to use colour with a special camera. After this, Walt made all his films in colour.

Mickey Mouse **cartoons** were very popular with children and grown-ups. Walt began to sell toys, comics and watches using the Mickey Mouse name. This is called **merchandising**.

Music and films

In 1933, Walt began to use music in his **cartoons**. He recorded the music first and then made the cartoons move in time to the music. The *Three Little Pigs* was the first cartoon made like this.

At first, cartoons were very short. Then Walt started to make longer films like *Snow White and the Seven Dwarfs*, *Bambi*, *101 Dalmations* and *Mary Poppins*. He won 29 **Oscars** for his films.

Disneyland

Walt had many new ideas for **entertainment**. His next idea was to build a theme park for the whole family to enjoy. The first Disneyland opened in California in 1955, more than 40 years ago.

Walt wanted to open a second theme park called Disney World in Florida in 1966. He became ill and died just before it was finished. Many people were sad because they had enjoyed his work so much.

Walt Disney Company

There are many ways to find out about Walt Disney. You can see his **cartoons** at the cinema. His company still exists in America and makes films like *The Lion King* and *James and the Giant Peach*.

Theme parks

The Walt Disney Company also owns theme parks. After Walt died, Disneyland in Florida was opened. The newest theme park is Eurodisney, in France, near Paris.

Photographs

People took a lot of photos and made many films about Walt. This photo shows him appearing on television at a Mickey Mouse Club.

Posters

Walt used posters to show which of his films were on at the cinema. Here is a poster for *Pinocchio*.

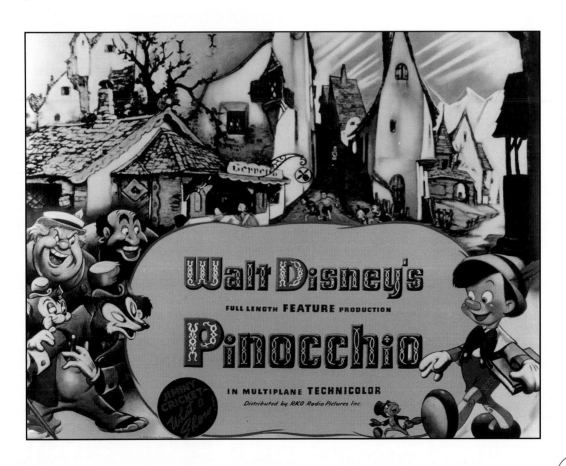

Newspapers

There were so many stories in the newspapers about Walt's life and work. We can still read them today.

Books

There are many books we can read about Walt's life and work. This book tells us how he made his **cartoons**.

Disney Stores

There are many new Disney Stores all over the world. These shops sell books, toys and videos about Walt and his **cartoon characters**.

Disney Street

There is a street in London called Disney Street. This shows how important people think Walt Disney is. Here is a photo of him and his wife Lily, in Disney Street.

Glossary

This glossary explains difficult words, and helps you to say words which are hard to say.

animation a way of making a cartoon film: you draw a lot of cartoons or pictures that show the characters in slightly different positions, then you photograph each drawing and then play the photos quickly, one after the other – the cartoons look as if they are moving. You say *ani-may-shun*

cartoon a funny drawing or film of drawings

character a person or an animal in a film, story or play. You say *ka-rak-ter*

entertainment a way of getting people to have fun

merchandising selling things that have the name or picture of a well-known character or company on them. You say *mer-chan-di-zing*

Oscars prizes given in America for the best films made each year – each prize is a golden statue of a man. You say *oss-kerz*

studio a room used to record films

silent a film that has no sound in it

Index